POETRY FOR KIDS

Shakespeare

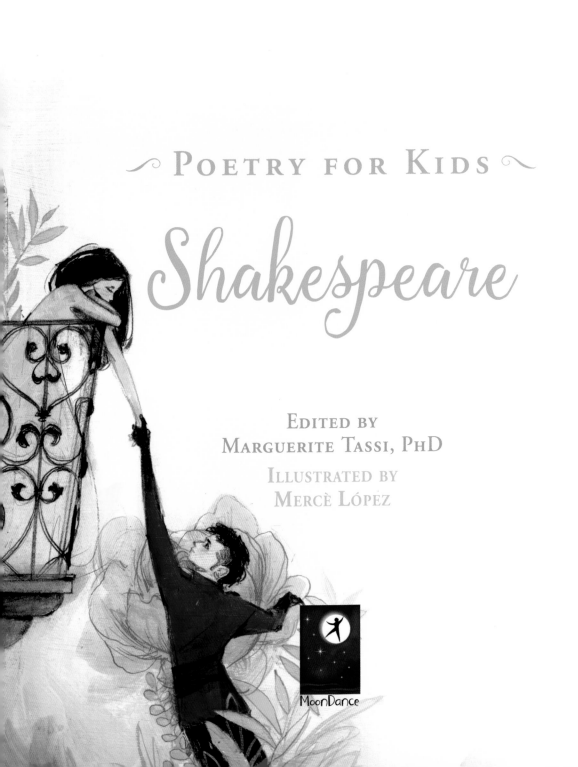

~ POETRY FOR KIDS ~

Shakespeare

EDITED BY
MARGUERITE TASSI, PhD

ILLUSTRATED BY
MERCÈ LÓPEZ

MoonDance

Brimming with creative inspiration, how-to projects, and useful information to enrich your everyday life, Quarto Knows is a favorite destination for those pursuing their interests and passions. Visit our site and dig deeper with our books into your area of interest: Quarto Creates, Quarto Cooks, Quarto Homes, Quarto Lives, Quarto Drives, Quarto Explores, Quarto Gifts, or Quarto Kids.

This book is dedicated to my wonderful children, Francesca and James. —M.T.

To Roberto and Frida —M.L.

First published in 2018 by MoonDance Press, an imprint of The Quarto Group.
26391 Crown Valley Parkway, Suite 220, Mission Viejo, CA 92691, USA.
T (949) 380-7510 **F** (949) 380-7575 **www.QuartoKnows.com**

MoonDance Press titles are also available at discount for retail, wholesale, promotional, and bulk purchase. For details, contact the Special Sales Manager by email at specialsales@quarto.com or by mail at The Quarto Group, Attn: Special Sales Manager, 100 Cummings Center, Suite 265D, Beverly, MA 01915, USA.

ISBN: 978-1-63322-504-6

Digital edition published in 2018
eISBN: 978-1-63322-505-3

Cover design and layout by Melissa Gerber

Printed in China
10 9 8 7 6 5 4

Contents

Introduction

WILLIAM SHAKESPEARE WAS AN ENGLISH PLAYWRIGHT, ACTOR, AND POET who lived during the reigns of two monarchs, Queen Elizabeth I and King James I. Widely regarded as the greatest writer in the English language, he has gained fame across the globe for his brilliance as a dramatist.

For all of his fame and fortune, William's beginnings were humble. He was born in April 1564 in Stratford, a small town on the River Avon one hundred miles from London. He was the oldest surviving child of John Shakespeare, a successful glove maker, and Mary Arden. William attended the King's New School in Stratford, taking classes six days a week, primarily in Latin grammar and literature, until about the age of fifteen. At age eighteen, William married a local girl, Anne Hathaway. They had three children: Susanna and twins named Judith and Hamnet. Sadly, Hamnet lived only to the age of eleven. By all appearances, William's life was relatively quiet until his mid-twenties when he left Stratford to try his fortune in the big city.

In the late 1580s, the London-area theatres were on the rise, teeming with excitement and life. William made his way to London to work in this vibrant artistic world, where a new show played every afternoon in gorgeously painted wooden playhouses. William got his start as an actor, but it did not take long for him to realize that his greatest talent lay in playwriting. He joined an acting company called the Lord Chamberlain's Men, later known as the King's Men (when James I became their patron). William became the company's resident dramatist at the Theatre, the first professionally built playhouse in London. The Lord Chamberlain's Men were a travelling company as well, which meant that William's plays were performed at inns, royal courts, universities, and in other English towns.

William first won fame with his history plays in the early 1590s, which brought the thrilling stories of England's kings to the stage. He then gained further popularity with comedies like *A Midsummer Night's Dream* and tragedies, such as *Romeo and Juliet* and *Hamlet*. His soaring poetry, lifelike characters, and dramatic innovations made William the most popular playwright of his time. He also earned a reputation as a poet, writing a number of long poems and 154 sonnets.

William is best known for his association with the Globe Theatre. When the Lord Chamberlain's Men lost their lease to the land under the Theatre, they took a risk that changed the course of history. In the dead of night, the men met at the Theatre, and despite the wintry cold, they worked to dismantle the entire building. Then they carried the timber across the frozen River Thames to another site, where the playhouse was rebuilt and named the Globe. Although it was demolished eventually in 1644, a new Globe playhouse was built many years later and opened in 1997.

William died a wealthy man in Stratford in April 1616 at the age of fifty-two. Seven years later, his friends from the King's Men, John Heminge and Henry Condell, did something that would change literary and theatrical history profoundly. They collected all of William's handwritten scripts and brought them to a printer. In 1623, the collected plays of Shakespeare, called the First Folio, appeared in print. Among the thirty-six plays were eighteen that would have been lost had they not appeared in the Folio, including some of William's best loved works: *Macbeth*, *Julius Caesar*, *As You Like It*, and *The Tempest*. As his friend and fellow dramatist Ben Jonson wrote, William "was not of an age, but for all time."

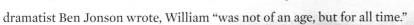

All the World's a Stage

FROM *As You Like It*, ACT 2, SCENE 7

All the world's a stage,
And all the men and women merely players:
They have their exits and their entrances,
And one man in his time plays many parts,
His acts being seven ages. At first the infant,
Mewling and puking in the nurse's arms.
And then the whining school-boy, with his satchel
And shining morning face, creeping like snail
Unwillingly to school. And then the lover,
Sighing like furnace, with a woeful ballad
Made to his mistress' eyebrow. Then a soldier,
Full of strange oaths and bearded like the pard,
Jealous in honour, sudden and quick in quarrel,
Seeking the bubble reputation
Even in the cannon's mouth. And then the justice,
In fair round belly with good capon lined,
With eyes severe and beard of formal cut,
Full of wise saws and modern instances;
And so he plays his part.

The sixth age shifts
Into the lean and slipper'd pantaloon,
With spectacles on nose and pouch on side,
His youthful hose, well saved, a world too wide
For his shrunk shank; and his big manly voice,
Turning again toward childish treble, pipes
And whistles in his sound. Last scene of all,
That ends this strange eventful history,
Is second childishness and mere oblivion,
Sans teeth, sans eyes, sans taste, sans everything.

Mewling—whimpering
Like furnace—like a furnace emitting smoke
Bearded like the pard—having whiskers like a leopard
Jealous in honour—carefully guarding his honour
Bubble reputation—fleeting glory
Capon—cock fattened for eating; often presented to judges as a bribe
Saws—sayings
Modern instances—commonplace illustrations or proofs against universal beliefs
Pantaloon—ridiculous old merchant from Italian comedy
Hose—leggings
A world—far
Shank—leg
Mere oblivion—complete forgetfulness
Sans—without

O, for a Muse of Fire

FROM *Henry V*, ACT 1, PROLOGUE

O, for a Muse of fire, that would ascend
The brightest heaven of invention,
A kingdom for a stage, princes to act
And monarchs to behold the swelling scene!
Then should the warlike Harry, like himself,
Assume the port of Mars; and at his heels,
Leash'd in like hounds, should famine, sword and fire
Crouch for employment. But pardon, and gentles all,
The flat unraised spirits that have dared
On this unworthy scaffold to bring forth
So great an object: can this cockpit hold
The vasty fields of France? or may we cram
Within this wooden O the very casques
That did affright the air at Agincourt?
O, pardon! since a crooked figure may
Attest in little place a million;
And let us, ciphers to this great accompt,

On your imaginary forces work.
Suppose within the girdle of these walls
Are now confined two mighty monarchies,
Whose high upreared and abutting fronts
The perilous Narrow Ocean parts asunder:
Piece out our imperfections with your thoughts;
Into a thousand parts divide one man,
And make imaginary puissance;
Think when we talk of horses, that you see them
Printing their proud hoofs i' th' receiving earth;
For 'tis your thoughts that now must deck our kings,
Carry them here and there; jumping o'er times,
Turning the accomplishment of many years
Into an hour-glass: for the which supply,
Admit me Chorus to this history;
Who Prologue-like your humble patience pray,
Gently to hear, kindly to judge, our play.

Muse—source of inspiration
Invention—imagination
Swelling—increasing in magnificence
Port—appearance
Scaffold—stage's platform
Wooden O—a circular amphitheatre
Very casque—actual helmets
Agincourt—a village in Northern France
  where Henry V won his greatest victory
Crooked figure—zero
Attest—stand for
Narrow Ocean—the English Channel
Ciphers—zeroes
Parts—actors' roles
Puissance—armies

Behind—to come

Changed—exchanged

Ill-doing—sin

Reared—raised

Weak spirits—youthful vital powers

Stronger blood—adult emotions, passions

The imposition cleared/ Hereditary ours—the burden of original sin is not ours. In Christianity, it was thought that humans were born with sin because Adam and Eve disobeyed God.

We Were, Fair Queen

FROM *The Winter's Tale*, ACT 1, SCENE 2

We were, fair Queen,
Two lads that thought there was no more behind
But such a day to-morrow as to-day,
And to be boy eternal.
We were as twinn'd lambs that did frisk i' th' sun,
And bleat the one at th' other. What we changed
Was innocence for innocence. We knew not
The doctrine of ill-doing, nor dream'd
That any did. Had we pursued that life,
And our weak spirits ne'er been higher rear'd
With stronger blood, we should have answer'd heaven
Boldly, 'Not guilty', the imposition clear'd
Hereditary ours.

Over Hill, Over Dale

FROM *A Midsummer Night's Dream*, ACT 2, SCENE 1

Over hill, over dale,
    Thorough bush, thorough briar,
Over park, over pale,
    Thorough flood, thorough fire,
I do wander everywhere,
Swifter than the moon's sphere;
And I serve the Fairy Queen,
To dew her orbs upon the green.
The cowslips tall her pensioners be:
In their gold coats spots you see;
Those be rubies, fairy favours,
In those freckles live their savours:
I must go seek some dewdrops here
And hang a pearl in every cowslip's ear.

Dale—a wide, open valley
Thorough—through
Pale—fenced-in area
Moon's sphere—In Ptolemaic
  astronomy, it was thought
  that the moon was carried
  around the earth in its own
  transparent crystal globe.
Orbs—circles of dark grass
  where fairies danced
Cowslips—yellow flowers
Pensioners—the royal
  bodyguards, dressed in bright
  colours
Savours—fragrance

Round About the Cauldron Go

FROM *Macbeth*, ACT 4, SCENE 1

Round about the cauldron go;
In the poison'd entrails throw.
Toad, that under cold stone
Days and nights has thirty-one
Swelter'd venom sleeping got,
Boil thou first i' th' charmed pot.

Double, double, toil and trouble;
Fire burn, and cauldron bubble.

Fillet of a fenny snake,
In the cauldron boil and bake.
Eye of newt, and toe of frog,
Wool of bat, and tongue of dog,
Adder's fork, and blind-worm's sting,
Lizard's leg, and owlet's wing,
For a charm of powerful trouble,
Like a hell-broth, boil and bubble.

Double, double, toil and trouble;
Fire burn, and cauldron bubble.

*Swelter'd venom sleeping got—releases poison
  formed during sleep*
Toil—hard work, dispute
Fillet—slice
Fenny—from the marshlands
Fork—poisonous split tongue
Blind-worm—an adder

Under the Greenwood Tree

FROM *As You Like It*, ACT 2, SCENE 5

Under the greenwood tree,
    Who loves to lie with me,
And turn his merry note
    Unto the sweet bird's throat;
Come hither, come hither, come hither:
    Here shall he see
    No enemy
But winter and rough weather.

Who doth ambition shun
    And loves to live i' th' sun,
Seeking the food he eats,
    And pleased with what he gets;
Come hither, come hither, come hither:
    Here shall he see
    No enemy
But winter and rough weather.

Turn—tune, adapt
Throat—voice
Live i' th' sun—free from care

Shall I Compare Thee to a Summer's Day?

SONNET 18

Shall I compare thee to a summer's day?
Thou art more lovely and more temperate:
Rough winds do shake the darling buds of May,
And summer's lease hath all too short a date:
Sometime too hot the eye of heaven shines,
And often is his gold complexion dimm'd;
And every fair from fair sometime declines,
By chance or nature's changing course untrimm'd;
But thy eternal summer shall not fade
Nor lose possession of that fair thou ow'st;
Nor shall Death brag thou wander'st in his shade,
When in eternal lines to time thou grow'st:
      So long as men can breathe or eyes can see,
      So long lives this, and this gives life to thee.

Temperate—mild
Lease—time allowed
Date—duration
The eye of heaven—the sun
Every fair from fair sometime declines—everything beautiful loses its beauty
Untrimm'd—stripped of its beauty
Ow'st—own
Lines—lines of poetry
Thou grow'st—you become part of the poem and, therefore, of time
This—the poem

O Romeo, Romeo, Wherefore Art Thou Romeo?

FROM *Romeo and Juliet*, ACT 2, SCENE 2

O Romeo, Romeo, wherefore art thou Romeo?
Deny thy father and refuse thy name;
Or, if thou wilt not, be but sworn my love,
And I'll no longer be a Capulet.
'Tis but thy name that is my enemy;
Thou art thyself, though not a Montague.
What's Montague? It is nor hand, nor foot,
Nor arm, nor face, nor any other part
Belonging to a man. O, be some other name!
What's in a name? That which we call a rose
By any other name would smell as sweet;
So Romeo would, were he not Romeo call'd,
Retain that dear perfection which he owes
Without that title. Romeo, doff thy name,
And for thy name which is no part of thee
Take all myself.

Wherefore—why
Though—even if
Owes—owns
Doff—cast aside

Now Is the Winter of Our Discontent

FROM *Richard III*, ACT 1, SCENE 1

Now is the winter of our discontent
Made glorious summer by this son of York;
And all the clouds that low'r'd upon our house
In the deep bosom of the ocean buried.
Now are our brows bound with victorious wreaths;
Our bruised arms hung up for monuments;
Our stern alarums changed to merry meetings,
Our dreadful marches to delightful measures.
Grim-visaged War hath smooth'd his wrinkled front;
And now, instead of mounting barbed steeds
To fright the souls of fearful adversaries,
He capers nimbly in a lady's chamber
To the lascivious pleasing of a lute.
But I, that am not shaped for sportive tricks,
Nor made to court an amorous looking-glass;
I, that am rudely stamp'd, and want love's majesty
To strut before a wanton ambling nymph;
I, that am curtail'd of this fair proportion,

Cheated of feature by dissembling nature,
Deformed, unfinish'd, sent before my time
Into this breathing world, scarce half made up,
And that so lamely and unfashionable
That dogs bark at me as I halt by them;
Why, I, in this weak piping time of peace,
Have no delight to pass away the time,
Unless to see my shadow in the sun
And descant on mine own deformity:
And therefore, since I cannot prove a lover,
To entertain these fair well-spoken days,
I am determined to prove a villain
And hate the idle pleasures of these days.

Son of York—in British history, Edward IV, son of Richard, Duke of York
Low'r'd—frowned
Bruised arms—battered weapons, armour
Alarums—summons to battle by drums and trumpets
Measures—melodies, stately dances
Wrinkled front—frowning forehead
Capers nimbly—leaps quickly and lightly in dance
Lascivious—desirable
Sportive tricks—playful games
Rudely stamped—roughly shaped
Want—lack
Wanton ambling—playfully strolling
Nymph—beautiful young woman
Curtailed—deprived
Feature—bodily shape
Dissembling—deceitful
Sent before my time—born prematurely
Piping—sounding like a pipe, or wind instrument
Descant—sing or play variations on a musical theme, comment on

If Music Be the Food of Love

FROM *Twelfth Night*, ACT 1, SCENE 1

If music be the food of love, play on;
Give me excess of it, that, surfeiting,
The appetite may sicken, and so die.
That strain again! it had a dying fall.
O, it came o'er my ear like the sweet sound
That breathes upon a bank of violets,
Stealing and giving odour! Enough; no more:
'Tis not so sweet now as it was before.
O spirit of love! how quick and fresh art thou,
That, notwithstanding thy capacity
Receiveth as the sea, nought enters there,
Of what validity and pitch so e'er,
But falls into abatement and low price,
Even in a minute! So full of shapes is fancy
That it alone is high fantastical.

Surfeiting—consuming too much
That strain again—(to the musicians)
  play that musical phrase again
Dying fall—fading away
Quick and fresh—alive and eager, hungry
Capacity/Receiveth as the sea—able to
  take in impressions as vast as the sea
Validity and pitch—high value
Abatement—decline
Shapes—imagined forms
Fancy—love
High fantastical—highly imaginative,
  very passionate

How Sweet the Moonlight Sleeps Upon This Bank!

FROM *The Merchant of Venice*, ACT 5, SCENE 1

How sweet the moonlight sleeps upon this bank!
Here will we sit and let the sounds of music
Creep in our ears: soft stillness and the night
Become the touches of sweet harmony.
Sit, Jessica. Look how the floor of heaven
Is thick inlaid with patens of bright gold:
There's not the smallest orb which thou behold'st
But in his motion like an angel sings,
Still quiring to the young-eyed cherubins;
Such harmony is in immortal souls;
But whilst this muddy vesture of decay
Doth grossly close it in, we cannot hear it.

Bank—a slope of land alongside a river
Become—suit
Touches—musical notes
Floor of heaven—the sky
Patens—shallow dishes
Motion of the orbs—the belief that the concentric circles of the Ptolemaic spheres created harmonious music by their movement (known as the music of the spheres), which cannot be heard by mortals
Still quiring—continually singing together
Cherubins—angels
Muddy vesture of decay—the body
Doth grossly close it in—does physically enclose an immortal soul

O, She Doth Teach the Torches to Burn Bright!

FROM *Romeo and Juliet*, ACT 1, SCENE 5

O, she doth teach the torches to burn bright!

It seems she hangs upon the cheek of night

Like a rich jewel in an Ethiope's ear;

Beauty too rich for use, for earth too dear!

So shows a snowy dove trooping with crows,

As yonder lady o'er her fellows shows.

The measure done, I'll watch her place of stand,

And, touching hers, make blessed my rude hand.

Did my heart love till now? forswear it, sight!

For I ne'er saw true beauty till this night.

Doth—does
Ethiope—Ethiopian, black African
*Beauty too rich for use, for earth too dear—beauty that is too precious for this
    world*
Trooping—flocking
Measure—dance
Forswear—break a former oath

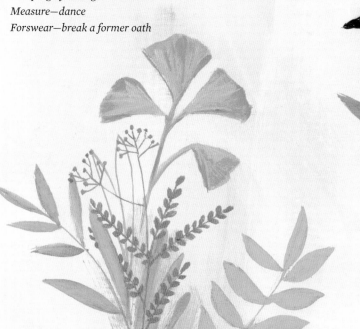

O Mistress Mine, Where Are You Roaming?

FROM *Twelfth Night*, ACT 2, SCENE 3

O mistress mine, where are you roaming?
O, stay and hear; your true love's coming,
 That can sing both high and low.
Trip no further, pretty sweeting;
Journeys end in lovers meeting,
 Every wise man's son doth know.

What is love? 'Tis not hereafter;
Present mirth hath present laughter;
 What's to come is still unsure.
In delay there lies no plenty;
Then come kiss me, sweet and twenty;
 Youth's a stuff will not endure.

Mistress—girlfriend, beloved
Still—always
Sweet and twenty—sweet and twenty times sweet

24

What Light Is Light, if Silvia Be Not Seen?

FROM *The Two Gentlemen of Verona*, ACT 3, SCENE 1

What light is light, if Silvia be not seen?
What joy is joy, if Silvia be not by?
Unless it be to think that she is by
And feed upon the shadow of perfection
Except I be by Silvia in the night,
There is no music in the nightingale;
Unless I look on Silvia in the day,
There is no day for me to look upon.

Shadow—image

But Soft, What Light Through Yonder Window Breaks?

FROM *Romeo and Juliet*, ACT 2, SCENE 2

But soft, what light through yonder window breaks?

It is the east, and Juliet is the sun.

Arise, fair sun, and kill the envious moon,

Who is already sick and pale with grief,

That thou her maid art far more fair than she:

Be not her maid, since she is envious;

Her vestal livery is but sick and green

And none but fools do wear it; cast it off.

It is my lady, O, it is my love!

O, that she knew she were!

She speaks yet she says nothing: what of that?

Her eye discourses; I will answer it.

I am too bold, 'tis not to me she speaks:

Two of the fairest stars in all the heaven,

Having some business, do entreat her eyes

To twinkle in their spheres till they return.

What if her eyes were there, they in her head?

The brightness of her cheek would shame those stars,

As daylight doth a lamp; her eyes in heaven

Would through the airy region stream so bright

That birds would sing and think it were not night.

See, how she leans her cheek upon her hand!

O, that I were a glove upon that hand,

That I might touch that cheek!

Soft—wait
*Her maid—a follower of Diana,
  goddess of the moon*
*Vestal livery—pure clothing,
  appearance*
*Sick and green—anemia suffered by
  young girls, paleness*
Discourses—speaks
Stars—planets
There—in the stars' spheres
Airy region—heavens

My Mistress' Eyes Are Nothing Like the Sun

SONNET 130

My mistress' eyes are nothing like the sun;
Coral is far more red than her lips' red;
If snow be white, why then her breasts are dun;
If hairs be wires, black wires grow on her head.
I have seen roses damask'd, red and white,
But no such roses see I in her cheeks;
And in some perfumes is there more delight
Than in the breath that from my mistress reeks.
I love to hear her speak, yet well I know
That music hath a far more pleasing sound;
I grant I never saw a goddess go;
My mistress, when she walks, treads on the ground.
    And yet, by heaven, I think my love as rare
    As any she belied with false compare.

Dun—dull grey-brown
Damask'd—ornamented with streaks of color
Reeks—exhales (not necessarily an unpleasant smell)
Go—walk
Rare—special
Any she belied with false compare—any woman lied about in poetry

28

The Lunatic, the Lover, and the Poet

FROM *A Midsummer Night's Dream*, ACT 5, SCENE 1

The lunatic, the lover, and the poet

Are of imagination all compact.

One sees more devils than vast hell can hold:

That is the madman. The lover, all as frantic,

Sees Helen's beauty in a brow of Egypt.

The poet's eye, in a fine frenzy rolling,

Doth glance from heaven to earth, from earth to heaven,

And, as imagination bodies forth

The forms of things unknown, the poet's pen

Turns them to shapes, and gives to airy nothing

A local habitation and a name.

Such tricks hath strong imagination,

That if it would but apprehend some joy,

It comprehends some bringer of that joy;

Or in the night, imagining some fear,

How easy is a bush supposed a bear!

Compact—composed
Helen's beauty—alluding to the legendary beauty of the blonde and
  fair-skinned Helen of Troy
A brow of Egypt—the dark-complexioned face of a woman from Egypt
Airy nothing—the insubstantial stuff of the imagination
Local habitation—through writing, the poet creates a place for the
  imagination to take form.
Apprehend—imagine
Bringer—the source

29

Let Me Not to the Marriage of True Minds

SONNET 116

Let me not to the marriage of true minds
Admit impediments. Love is not love
Which alters when it alteration finds,
Or bends with the remover to remove.
O no! it is an ever-fixed mark
That looks on tempests and is never shaken;
It is the star to every wand'ring bark,
Whose worth's unknown, although his height be taken.
Love's not Time's fool, though rosy lips and cheeks
Within his bending sickle's compass come:
Love alters not with his brief hours and weeks,
But bears it out even to the edge of doom.
    If this be error and upon me proved,
    I never writ, nor no man ever loved.

Let me not—may I never
Admit impediments—allow objections (referring to the marriage service)
Bends with the remover to remove—inclining to change affections when the beloved does
Ever-fixed mark—a signal or beacon for ships to aid in navigation
Star—the guiding North Star
Wand'ring bark—lost ship
Whose worth's unknown—the value of which is beyond human measurement
His height be taken—altitude scientifically measured
Time's fool—something mocked by Time because Time has power over it
His bending sickle—the image of Time, like Death the Reaper, with a curved-edged farming tool
Upon me proved—proved against me

Cowards Die Many Times Before Their Deaths

FROM *Julius Caesar*, ACT 2, SCENE 2

Cowards die many times before their deaths;
The valiant never taste of death but once.
Of all the wonders that I yet have heard,
It seems to me most strange that men should fear,
Seeing that death, a necessary end,
Will come when it will come.

Once More Unto the Breach

FROM *Henry V*, ACT 3, SCENE 1

Once more unto the breach, dear friends, once more;
Or close the wall up with our English dead.
In peace there's nothing so becomes a man
As modest stillness and humility,
But when the blast of war blows in our ears,
Then imitate the action of the tiger.
Stiffen the sinews, conjure up the blood,
Disguise fair nature with hard-favour'd rage.
Then lend the eye a terrible aspect;
Let it pry through the portage of the head
Like the brass cannon; let the brow o'erwhelm it
As fearfully as doth a galled rock
O'erhang and jutty his confounded base,
Swill'd with the wild and wasteful ocean.
Now set the teeth and stretch the nostril wide,
Hold hard the breath, and bend up every spirit
To his full height. . .
I see you stand like greyhounds in the slips,
Straining upon the start. The game's afoot.
Follow your spirit, and upon this charge
Cry 'God for Harry, England and Saint George!'

Breach—a gap in a wall made by an attacking army
Fair nature—naturally handsome appearance
Hard-favour'd—stern-faced
Aspect—look
Let it pry through the portage—let the eye look
  through its socket
O'erwhelm—overhang the eyes with frowning
Galled—worn
Jutty—project over

Confounded—worn away
Swill'd—vigorously washed
Greyhounds on the slips—hunting dogs on leashes
The game's afoot—the prey are running
Harry, England and Saint George—the standard
  battle cry for England's army; Saint George is
  England's patron saint.

All Furnish'd, All in Arms

FROM *Henry IV, Part 1,* ACT 4, SCENE 1

All furnish'd, all in arms;
All plumed like ostriches, that with the wind
Baited like eagles having lately bathed;
Glittering in golden coats like images;
As full of spirit as the month of May,
And gorgeous as the sun at midsummer;
Wanton as youthful goats, wild as young bulls.
I saw young Harry with his beaver on,
His cuisses on his thighs, gallantly arm'd
Rise from the ground like feather'd Mercury,
And vaulted with such ease into his seat,
As if an angel dropp'd down from the clouds,
To turn and wind a fiery Pegasus,
And witch the world with noble horsemanship.

Furnish'd—dressed
Plumed—referring to feathers in a helmet
Baited—beating their wings
Golden coats—richly embroidered garments worn over armour
Images—pictures or statues illuminated with gold
Wanton—frisky
Beaver—helmet
Cuisses—thigh armour
Feather'd Mercury—the messenger of the gods in Roman mythology, represented with wings on his heels and cap
Wind—wheel about
Pegasus—winged horse of Greek mythology
Witch—bewitch

34

Strain'd—forced
Becomes—dignifies, graces
Sceptre—the monarch's staff,
  symbol of power
Temporal—earthly
Attribute to—outward show of
Seasons—softens

The Quality of Mercy Is Not Strain'd

FROM *The Merchant of Venice*, ACT 4, SCENE 1

The quality of mercy is not strain'd.
It droppeth as the gentle rain from heaven
Upon the place beneath. It is twice blest:
It blesseth him that gives, and him that takes.
'Tis mightiest in the mightiest; it becomes
The throned monarch better than his crown.
His sceptre shows the force of temporal power,
The attribute to awe and majesty,
Wherein doth sit the dread and fear of kings;
But mercy is above this sceptred sway.
It is enthroned in the hearts of kings;
It is an attribute to God himself;
And earthly power doth then show likest God's
When mercy seasons justice.

Friends, Romans, Countrymen, Lend Me Your Ears

FROM *Julius Caesar,* ACT 3, SCENE 2

Friends, Romans, countrymen, lend me your ears.
I come to bury Caesar, not to praise him.
The evil that men do lives after them;
The good is oft interred with their bones.
So let it be with Caesar. The noble Brutus
Hath told you Caesar was ambitious.
If it were so, it was a grievous fault,
And grievously hath Caesar answer'd it.
Here, under leave of Brutus and the rest
(For Brutus is an honourable man,
So are they all, all honourable men),
Come I to speak in Caesar's funeral.
He was my friend, faithful and just to me.
But Brutus says he was ambitious,
And Brutus is an honourable man.

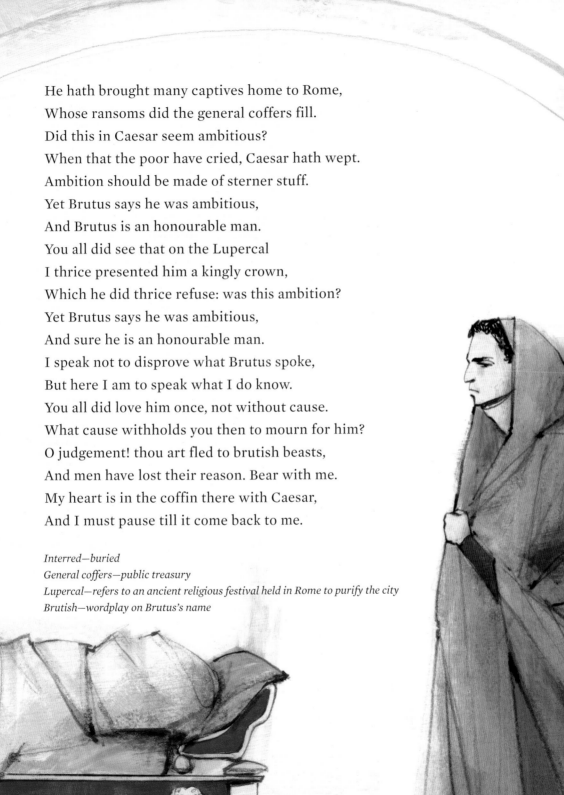

He hath brought many captives home to Rome,

Whose ransoms did the general coffers fill.

Did this in Caesar seem ambitious?

When that the poor have cried, Caesar hath wept.

Ambition should be made of sterner stuff.

Yet Brutus says he was ambitious,

And Brutus is an honourable man.

You all did see that on the Lupercal

I thrice presented him a kingly crown,

Which he did thrice refuse: was this ambition?

Yet Brutus says he was ambitious,

And sure he is an honourable man.

I speak not to disprove what Brutus spoke,

But here I am to speak what I do know.

You all did love him once, not without cause.

What cause withholds you then to mourn for him?

O judgement! thou art fled to brutish beasts,

And men have lost their reason. Bear with me.

My heart is in the coffin there with Caesar,

And I must pause till it come back to me.

Interred—buried
General coffers—public treasury
Lupercal—refers to an ancient religious festival held in Rome to purify the city
Brutish—wordplay on Brutus's name

All That Glitters Is Not Gold

FROM *The Merchant of Venice*, ACT 2, SCENE 7

All that glitters is not gold;
Often have you heard that told.
Many a man his life hath sold
But my outside to behold.
Gilded tombs do worms enfold.

But my outside—only the exterior gold
Gilded—glittering with gold
Tombs do worms infold—tombs enclose worms

That Time of Year Thou Mayst in Me Behold

SONNET 73

That time of year thou mayst in me behold,
When yellow leaves, or none, or few, do hang
Upon those boughs which shake against the cold,
Bare ruin'd choirs where late the sweet birds sang.
In me thou seest the twilight of such day
As after sunset fadeth in the west,
Which by and by black night doth take away,
Death's second self that seals up all in rest.
In me thou seest the glowing of such fire
That on the ashes of his youth doth lie,
As the death-bed whereon it must expire,
Consumed with that which it was nourish'd by.
    This thou perceiv'st, which makes thy love more strong,
    To love that well, which thou must leave ere long.

Bare ruin'd choirs—the tree's branches imagined as
* bare, without the singing birds of spring and summer*
Death's second self—sleep

39

To Be, or Not to Be, That Is the Question

FROM *Hamlet,* ACT 3, SCENE 1

To be, or not to be, that is the question:
Whether 'tis nobler in the mind to suffer
The slings and arrows of outrageous fortune,
Or to take arms against a sea of troubles,
And by opposing end them. To die, to sleep—
No more; and by a sleep to say we end
The heart-ache and the thousand natural shocks
That flesh is heir to; 'tis a consummation
Devoutly to be wish'd. To die, to sleep—
To sleep, perchance to dream. Ay, there's the rub;
For in that sleep of death what dreams may come
When we have shuffled off this mortal coil,
Must give us pause. There's the respect
That makes calamity of so long life.
For who would bear the whips and scorns of time,
Th' oppressor's wrong, the proud man's contumely,
The pangs of despised love, the law's delay,
The insolence of office, and the spurns
That patient merit of th' unworthy takes,
When he himself might his quietus make
With a bare bodkin? Who would fardels bear,
To grunt and sweat under a weary life,
But that the dread of something after death,
The undiscover'd country from whose bourn
No traveller returns, puzzles the will,
And makes us rather bear those ills we have

Than fly to others that we know not of?
Thus conscience does make cowards of us all;
And thus the native hue of resolution
Is sicklied o'er with the pale cast of thought,
And enterprises of great pitch and moment
With this regard their currents turn awry,
And lose the name of action. Soft you now,
The fair Ophelia? Nymph, in thy orisons
Be all my sins remember'd.

Outrageous—violent, cruel
Consummation—an ending
Rub—obstacle
Shuffled off this mortal coil—to die
Respect—consideration
Contumely—contempt
Office—people who hold an office
Spurns—scornful rejections
Quietus—release
Bare bodkin—a mere dagger
Fardels—burdens
Bourn—boundary
Native hue—natural colour
Cast—shade, tint
Pitch—aspiration, scope
Moment—importance
Turn awry—turning away from its course
Soft you—wait a moment
Orisons—prayers

Blow, Winds, and Crack Your Cheeks!

FROM *King Lear*, ACT 3, SCENE 2

Blow, winds, and crack your cheeks! Rage, blow,
You cataracts and hurricanoes, spout
Till you have drench'd our steeples, drown'd the cocks!
You sulph'rous and thought-executing fires,
Vaunt-couriers to oak-cleaving thunderbolts,
Singe my white head! And thou, all-shaking thunder,
Smite flat the thick rotundity o' the world!
Crack nature's moulds, all germens spill at once,
That make ingrateful man!

*Crack your cheeks—winds personified
   as faces with puffed-out cheeks*
Cataracts—floodgates of the heavens
Hurricanoes—water spouts
Drench'd—submerged
*Cocks—weathervanes at the top of
   church steeples*
*Thought-executing fires—lightning
   (quick as thought)*
Vaunt-couriers—forerunners
*Smite flat—hit with great force
   (flatten)*
*Crack nature's moulds—destroy the
   molds that nature uses to create
   humans*
Germens—seeds
Spill—destroy
Ingrateful—ungrateful

To-morrow, and To-morrow, and To-morrow

FROM *Macbeth*, ACT 5, SCENE 5

To-morrow, and to-morrow, and to-morrow
Creeps in this petty pace from day to day
To the last syllable of recorded time;
And all our yesterdays have lighted fools
The way to dusty death. Out, out, brief candle!
Life's but a walking shadow, a poor player
That struts and frets his hour upon the stage
And then is heard no more. It is a tale
Told by an idiot, full of sound and fury,
Signifying nothing.

Petty—meaningless
Syllable—merest trace
Poor player—bad actor
Frets—consumes

Why, Man, He Doth Bestride the Narrow World

FROM *Julius Caesar*, ACT 1, SCENE 2

Why, man, he doth bestride the narrow world
Like a Colossus, and we petty men
Walk under his huge legs and peep about
To find ourselves dishonourable graves.
Men at some time are masters of their fates.
The fault, dear Brutus, is not in our stars,
But in ourselves, that we are underlings.

Bestride—straddle
Colossus—legendary giant statue
*Stars—astrological influences that were
  thought to determine fate*

If We Shadows Have Offended

FROM *A Midsummer Night's Dream*, ACT 5, SCENE 1

If we shadows have offended,
Think but this, and all is mended,
That you have but slumber'd here
While these visions did appear.
And this weak and idle theme,
No more yielding but a dream,
Gentles, do not reprehend.
If you pardon, we will mend,
And, as I am an honest Puck,
If we have unearned luck
Now to 'scape the serpent's tongue,
We will make amends ere long;
Else the Puck a liar call.
So, good night unto you all.
Give me your hands, if we be friends,
And Robin shall restore amends.

Shadows—actors
No more yielding but a dream—with no more substance
   than a dream
Gentles—the audience
Reprehend—express disapproval
Mend—improve
'Scape the serpent's tongue—escape hissing
   from the audience
Give me your hands—applaud

Our Revels Now Are Ended

FROM *The Tempest,* ACT 4, SCENE 1

Our revels now are ended. These our actors,
As I foretold you, were all spirits and
Are melted into air, into thin air;
And, like the baseless fabric of this vision,
The cloud-capp'd towers, the gorgeous palaces,
The solemn temples, the great globe itself,
Yea, all which it inherit, shall dissolve,
And, like this insubstantial pageant faded,
Leave not a rack behind. We are such stuff
As dreams are made on, and our little life
Is rounded with a sleep.

Revels—the dance at the end of courtly entertainments
Baseless fabric—without substance
Globe—the world (alluding to the Globe Theatre)
Which it inherit—all those who occupy the earth
Pageant—scene, performance
Rack—cloud
Made on—made of
Rounded—surrounded

What William Was Thinking

All the World's a Stage: Theatre is the inspiration for this vision of the seven ages of man. In humorous detail, a parade of players appears, from the puking infant to the senile old man.

O, for a Muse of Fire: In the prologue to a history play featuring King Harry's conquest of France, an actor calls for inspiration. He asks the audience to use their imaginations to help fill in what the theater cannot show, such as vast fields of war.

We Were, Fair Queen: Two kings are remembering their childhood days when they were innocent and thought they would be boys forever.

Over Hill, Over Dale: Robin Goodfellow—a woodland elf from English folklore—travels the countryside serving the Fairy Queen, spreading dew on the grass and in the flowers.

Round About the Cauldron Go: Three witches brew up a powerful spell over their cauldron.

Under the Greenwood Tree: This lovely song invites us to celebrate a carefree life in nature.

Shall I Compare Thee to a Summer's Day: A poet wants to compare the beauty of his beloved to a summer's day. However, he realizes that summer can be unpleasant and that the seasons change. He envisions his love's beauty as an "eternal summer," which continually renews itself every time someone reads this poem.

O Romeo, Romeo, Wherefore Art Thou Romeo?: Juliet questions why she and Romeo must be bound to their names. Because their families are feuding (Capulets versus Montague), their names identify them as enemies. Juliet wishes that Romeo could discard his name so they could be together.

Now Is the Winter of Our Discontent: Richard, Duke of Gloucester, celebrates the victory of his family, the Yorks, in the Wars of the Roses. But when he thinks of his physical deformity, he feels bitter and decides to play the villain. Through violence, he will rise in power to become the infamous Richard III.

If Music Be the Food of Love: A lovesick man laments how music cannot cure him of his romantic passion. However, he compares the spirit of love to the sea.

How Sweet the Moonlight Sleeps Upon this Bank!: A young man and his love look at the beauty of the moonlit sky. He imagines that they can hear heavenly music in the night.

O, She Doth Teach the Torches to Burn Bright!: When Romeo catches his first glimpse of Juliet, he falls in love. Overwhelmed by her beauty, he imagines her as a bright light, a rich jewel, and a snowy dove.

O Mistress Mine, Where Are You Roaming?: This song celebrates the journey of love, which is best experienced when one is young.

What Light Is Light, If Silvia Be Not Seen?: A young man expresses such intense love that everything pales in the absence of his beloved. The best he can do is satisfy himself with the thought of her, which is just a "shadow" of the woman herself.

But Soft, What Light Through Yonder Window Breaks?: Romeo sees Juliet on her balcony. He imagines her as a brilliant source of light in the dark. She is the rising sun, more beautiful and vibrant than the pale moon, and her eyes are stars that might light up the sky.

My Mistress' Eyes Are Nothing Like the Sun: A poet creates a playful sonnet that mocks traditional love poems. Instead of praising his lady, he "dispraises" all of her parts. In the end, he declares his beloved just as "rare" as any of the ladies praised in poetry, which is the closest he comes to a declaration of love.

The Lunatic, the Lover, and the Poet: Imagination is a quality shared by madmen, lovers, and poets, who all see things that are not visible to the rational mind. The poet's genius lies in creating something out of nothing and giving it a name and a place to live in poetry and drama.

Let Me Not to the Marriage of True Minds: In this sonnet, the poet makes a declaration of true love, which remains constant in a world of change. In the final lines, the poet offers himself—and his poem—as proof that true love exists.

Cowards Die Many Times Before Their Deaths: Julius Caesar condemns cowards and praises the valiant who recognize that death is not to be feared.

Once More Unto the Breach: In his war against France, King Harry rouses his men to battle. He calls upon them to imitate the ferocity of a tiger.

All Furnish'd, All in Arms: This speech praises Harry (then a prince, soon to be king) by admiring his splendid armor and noble horsemanship.

The Quality of Mercy Is Not Strain'd: In William's play *The Merchant of Venice*, a young woman disguises herself as a lawyer to argue a case against a vengeful moneylender. Mercy, she declares, is a divine quality that blesses the giver and the receiver. Kings have earthly power, but they are most like God when they show mercy.

Friends, Romans, Countrymen, Lend Me Your Ears: In his funeral oration for Julius Caesar, Mark Antony refutes Brutus's accusation that Caesar was ambitious for the throne, and therefore deserved to be assassinated.

All That Glitters Is Not Gold: This wise saying reflects on how easily men are fooled by gold and exterior shows of wealth. Men have lost their lives in pursuit of all that dazzles the eye.

That Time of Year Thou Mayst in Me Behold: An aging poet using images of decay—the bare tree in winter, a fading sunset, and a dying fire—to acknowledge how strong his friend's love must be as the poet approaches his death.

To Be, or Not to Be, That Is the Question: Hamlet's contemplation of life and death is the most famous speech in theatre history. He fears what is to come in the afterlife and therefore hesitates to take his own life.

Blow, Winds, and Crack Your Cheeks!: Standing in the middle of a violent storm, King Lear calls upon the rain, thunder, and lightning to rage just as he is raging at the ingratitude of his daughters.

To-morrow, and To-morrow, and To-morrow: At his bleakest moment, Macbeth sees his life as a procession of meaningless days. He imagines himself as an actor playing his part for an hour on the stage, and then exiting to be heard no more.

Why, Man, He Doth Bestride the Narrow World: This vision of Julius Caesar as a gigantic statue whose legs straddle the world renders all of his followers as little, insignificant men. Cassius counsels Brutus to master his own destiny, rather than believe in the "stars" (fate).

If We Shadows Have Offended: Robin Goodfellow, a mischievous elf also known as Puck, speaks these final lines to the audience of *A Midsummer Night's Dream*, apologizing for anything in the play the actors ("shadows") have done that seemed offensive. He asks them to regard the play as nothing more than a dream.

Our Revels Now Are Ended: In William's last play, *The Tempest*, he reflects on how theatre is like life. Prospero, a mighty magician, has conjured spirits to perform a scene, and now that he has dismissed them, they disappear without a trace. So too, our brief life vanishes like a dream.

Index